Try to Feel It MY *Way*

Other Books by Suzette Haden Elgin

NONFICTION

Genderspeak: Men, Women, and the Gentle Art of Verbal Self-Defense
The Gentle Art of Verbal Self-Defense
More on the Gentle Art of Verbal Self-Defense
The Last Word on the Gentle Art of Verbal Self-Defense
Success with the Gentle Art of Verbal Self-Defense
Staying Well with the Gentle Art of Verbal Self-Defense
The Gentle Art of Written Self-Defense
You Can't *Say* That to Me!
BusinessSpeak: Using the Gentle Art of Persuasion to Get What You Want at Work
The Gentle Art of Communicating with Kids

TEXTBOOKS

Guide to Transformational Grammar (with John Grinder, Ph.D.)
Pouring Down Words
What Is Linguistics?

NOVELS

The Communipaths
Furthest
At the Seventh Level
Twelve Fair Kingdoms
The Grand Jubilee
And Then There'll Be Fireworks
Star-Anchored, Star-Angered
Native Tongue
Yonder Comes the Other End of Time
Native Tongue II: The Judas Rose
Native Tongue III: Earthsong

Audio Programs by Suzette Haden Elgin

Mastering the Gentle Art of Verbal Self-Defense
Success with the Gentle Art of Verbal Self-Defense
The Gentle Art of Verbal Self-Defense for Parents and Kids (with Rebecca Haden, M.A.)
The Gentle Art of Verbal Self-Defense for Parents and Teenagers (with Rebecca Haden, M.A.)

Try to Feel It MY Way

New Help for Touch Dominant People and Those Who Care About Them

Suzette Haden Elgin, Ph.D.

John Wiley & Sons, Inc.

New York • Chichester • Brisbane • Toronto • Singapore • Weinheim

This text is printed on acid-free paper.

Library of Congress Cataloging-in-Publication Data

Elgin, Suzette Haden.
Try to feel it my way : new help for touch dominant people and those who care about them / Suzette Haden Elgin.
p. cm.
Includes bibliographical references and index.
ISBN 0-471-00669-6 (alk. paper). — ISBN 0-471-00670-X (pbk. : alk. paper)
1. Touch. 2. Touch—Social aspects. 3. Nonverbal communication (Psychology) I. Title.
BF275.E44 1996
152.1'82—dc20 96-15553
CIP

Printed in the United States of America

10 9 8 7 6 5 4 3 2 1

Contents

Preface

Everywhere you look today there are books and audio programs and seminars on dealing with "Difficult People." Bosses who never stop complaining and criticizing, no matter how good your work is. Relatives who always find a way to pick a fight, even when everybody present is determined not to let it happen. Colleagues who aren't happy unless everybody else is miserable. Employees that nobody can talk to without feeling insulted and infuriated. Kids who whine and sulk and have no friends. JERKS . . . the people you duck into doorways to hide from if you can, because even a few minutes with them leaves your head pounding and your stomach churning. We all know and dread these people. (Some of us *are* these people, and have to live with the knowledge that others find us hard to get along with.)

This book won't give you yet another set of tips for easing your encounters with difficult people. Instead, I'm going to demonstrate to you that many "difficult people" aren't difficult at all. They behave the way they do because they are reacting much as you would react if you found yourself forced to use a foreign language for understanding and learning and communicating. These people aren't difficult—they're *touch dominant*. You may never have heard that phrase before; let me explain.

By the time children get to be five or six years old, they discover that one of our major sensory systems (sight or hearing or touch) *works* better for them than the others do. And just as their being right- or left-handed does not change, this dominant sense will not change. The sight dominant, for whom what matters is how things *look*, will have an advantage, because sight is the sense our culture values most. The hearing dominant, for whom what matters is how things *sound*, are somewhat less advantaged, but they'll still do all right. The majority—the Eye Tribe—are willing to agree that hearing also has importance and significance.

But what about people for whom the most important sense is *touch*? For touch dominant persons of *all* ages, information for the eyes and the ears isn't enough. To understand and learn and remember, they need information for the *flesh*. When they are tense or upset, they need to use the words and body language that go with touching, the vocabulary of the skin and the gut. (Do "information for the *flesh*" and "vocabulary of the skin and the gut" make you uneasy? Why? They're neither obscene nor inflammatory. Stay tuned.) We cut these individuals no slack in our culture, and the result is their most constant lament: "I just don't get it!"

Think about it: What would it be like to be touch dominant?

Imagine being someone whose dominant sense is touch, in a "Don't TOUCH!" society like ours where everything that matters most to you—down to the very words and body language you use under stress—is rejected by others. How would you manage? How good would your "people skills" be? Might you not rub people the wrong way and earn the label "difficult" for *yourself*?

This book will take you into the world of touch dominance and help you understand that world, alien as it may seem at first. It will help you understand the language of touch dominance, which is not as different from your language as Chinese or Cherokee but is still a communication barrier, and a barrier that's highest in anxious moments when good communication is the one thing most desperately needed. I will show you that when "difficult" is really "touch dominant," a set of simple language techniques can bring about changes that seem almost miraculous. Strange as the whole idea of touch dominance may be to you now, by the time you reach the end of this book, I promise you: You will "get it." And if you are yourself a touch dominant person, you will find yourself, for perhaps the first time, understanding why "getting it" is often so hard for *you*.

How to Use this Book

Chapter One is an introduction to the concept of touch dominance and its role in our lives. In Chapter Two we'll consider what life is like for touch dominant children and what problems it typically causes for them; Chapter Three covers that same territory for touch dominant adults. Chapters Four and Five offer ways to help with the problems; Chapter Six speaks directly to the touch dominant reader. Chapter Seven takes up the very special and thorny problems that touch dominance can cause for adults in their most intimate relationships.

The chapters contain dialogues and scenarios that show how touch dominance can lead to turmoil and communication breakdown—together with techniques for handling those consequences, and rewrites that demonstrate how applying the suggestions can make more positive outcomes possible. In addition, they include workout sections with additional materials that give you opportunities to use and expand your new information and skills. The appendices supplement the text with a sampler of American Sign Language words and phrases and a touch language version of "Goldilocks and the Three Bears" for reading to TD children. Finally, the references and bibliography at the end of the book will take you to many more sources of information about touch and the language of touch, and the book's index will make it easy for you to find information quickly and conveniently.

You may want to just read through the book quickly to get a basic understanding of its subject; or you may want to do the workout sections as you go along, to deepen your understanding. Either way, you'll notice something unusual: In *this* book, when a choice exists between a word or phrase in touch language and one that comes from the vocabulary of sight or hearing, I've tried always to use the touch item, even when it would not be the choice a teacher of English composition (or my editors) would consider best.

That's fair—because almost everything else you read in English will make the opposite choice, in order to *avoid* touch language. It's also useful, because your reaction to my choices will get my message across to you in a way that nothing else could. If you are touch dominant yourself, you will be reading a book that (as far as is possible for English) is put together using *your* language, for once. If you're not touch dominant, your negative reactions—"Goodness, what a crude way to put that!" and "Why in the world did she use such a colloquialism?" and "That doesn't sound very educated to me!"—will bring home to you forcefully how biased our culture is against everything that has to do with touch and the language of touch.

I could not have written this book without the help of many other people—far more than I have room to list here. I am especially grateful to the thousands of people who have responded to my writing and speaking about touch dominance by sharing with me their own ideas and stories of their own experiences as (or with) TD persons. On the list of people whose names I *do* have to set down here are . . . My graduate adviser, Leonard Newmark, who taught me how to make people want to learn and how to bring them through the learning experience successfully. Linguist John Grinder, who was my colleague in my earliest investigations of touch dominance and touch language. Virginia Satir and Edward T. Hall, who laid the foundations for much of my work with the subject.

My long-suffering family, on whom I can always count for support and tolerance. My editors at John Wiley & Sons, and especially senior editor PJ Dempsey and production editor Joanne Palmer.

To the many I have not named, and to those upon whose work I have built, my grateful thanks; to anyone I may have overlooked in spite of my best intentions, I sincerely apologize. The responsibility for mistakes and omissions must all be laid at my door.

If you have comments or questions, I would be pleased to hear from you. Feel free to write me directly, anytime; I will get back to you as quickly and fully as I can.

Suzette Haden Elgin, Ph.D.
P.O. Box 1137
Huntsville, Arkansas 72740-1137
E-mail: ocls@sibylline.com

Chapter One

A Rough Row to Hoe

Dialogue One
Between a Teacher and a Child

Child: "Mrs. Harper? I need some help—I don't get this!"

Teacher: "That's because you aren't even looking at it! How do you expect to learn anything that way? It's not written on the ceiling, you know! As usual—you're just not trying."

Child: "I am trying, but it's too hard! I just don't get it, that's all!"

Teacher: "Look, Sharon, I don't have time for this nonsense. You pay attention to your work, and don't let me see you staring out the window or up at the ceiling. Keep your eyes on your page and try again—and please don't bother me with any more of your ridiculous excuses!"

Dialogue Two

Between a Man and a Woman at the Office

Man: "Helen, I haven't seen those sales charts we asked you for yet. I'm sure it was clear that we wanted them as fast as possible. . . . Are they finished?"

Woman: "We don't need those charts, Jack."

Man: "Of course we need them! We have to be able to see our sales figures!"

Woman: "Jack, I can put my finger on any information we need, anytime. It's all right here in my head, and I can get at it a lot quicker than you can dig it out of a bunch of charts and graphs!"

Man: "Oh. I see. As usual, Helen, you've decided not to cooperate with the rest of us."

✦

The teacher in Dialogue One believes that the student isn't trying—*as usual.* The salesman in Dialogue Two believes that his colleague is deliberately sabotaging the sales team's efforts—*as usual.* Are they right?

Maybe so. Certainly there are youngsters who dislike school and won't do much more than keep their desks warm if they can get away with it. And there *are* adults who are just contrary and who seem to enjoy making life difficult for everyone around them. But there's another possibility. It may be that the student and the saleswoman in the dialogues are nothing at all like the images the teacher and the salesman have of them. It may be that they are both *touch dominant.* Let's look at a more detailed example of the kind of communication problems that touch dominance can lead to; look at Scenario One, please.

Scenario One

"Carolyn, I do not see why you won't at least try to help me a little!" said Mary Whitney. "You're not a baby, you're fifteen years old! Can't you see that this is important?"

Carolyn shrugged, and mumbled a quick "Sorry," but she didn't look up from her plate, and she didn't stop eating.

"Carolyn!" said her father sharply. "Will you please look at your mother when she talks to you?!"

The teenager put down her knife and fork, sighing, and did as she was told. "Okay, Mom," she said. "What do you want me to do?"

"One simple little thing," Mary answered. "Just tell me what color you want your room to *be*, that's all. The painters will be here tomorrow—I can't wait any longer."

Carolyn shrugged her shoulders again, slouching in her chair. "I don't care, Mom," she said.

"Oh, Carolyn! Not again!"

Mary turned to Frank, completely at the end of her patience. "See?" she demanded. "You see what I mean?"

"Sure," Frank said. "Sure I see—and it's clear that she has no intention of helping you. You ought to be used to that by now." He stood up and pushed back his chair, setting his coffee cup down in its saucer. "I'll leave you to it, honey," he said, "and I wish you luck; I have to leave or I'll be late. But this is the way she *always* is, Mary; I don't see why you're surprised."

When Frank had gone, Mary stared sadly at her daughter. "Well," she said slowly, "I guess I'll have to pick the color myself. I don't see any other way to solve this."

"That's okay, Mom," the girl said. "That's fine with me."

"But it's your room, Carolyn! You're the one who has to look at it all the time!"

Carolyn frowned, blinking fiercely to keep back the tears, and wrapped her arms tightly around her shoulders, hugging herself hard. "I don't get it," she said miserably. "Now what did I do wrong?"

✦

What's Going on Here?

This is a sad scene, but it's not unusual. When only one member of a family or group is touch dominant, this kind of scene can be expected. The problem here is that the parents believe this is happening because their daughter is deliberately refusing to cooperate and do her part in family projects. The problem is that this teenager doesn't know how to make her parents understand that that's not true, and has no idea how to explain. This is *communication breakdown.*

Mary and Frank Whitney are both sight dominant. They literally cannot *believe* that Carolyn is telling them the simple truth when she says "I don't care what color you paint my room." The way things *look* is so important to them that they can't imagine someone being indifferent about a color choice of that kind. Every time they ask their daughter to join in a discussion about visual things, however, the end result is the same: Both parents are angry, and the child is miserable and bewildered.

It seems to Carolyn that saying "Whatever you want to do is okay with me" *is* cooperating. It seems to her that she's always getting in trouble for telling the truth and for doing exactly what they're asking her to do. But it seems to her parents that she is an uncooperative, stubborn, annoying child who goes out of her way to be hard to get along with.

Suppose the parents are mistaken. Suppose that touch dominance is at the heart of this ongoing misunderstanding. What does that mean?

What Is Touch Dominance?

All human beings function in this world by processing information from the environment. We do this by using our *sensory systems*: sight and hearing and taste and smell and touch, plus perhaps as many as a dozen others that are less familiar. We use all our sensory systems that are in working order, to gather information and to handle it once it's gathered; we *need* them all.

When something stands in the way of using one sensory system, we fall back on the others to make up for it. Suppose you're exploring a cave and your only flashlight goes out and leaves you in total darkness. You don't just freeze where you are and give up all hope! You use your hands and feet to feel your way along. You listen as hard as you can for the clues your ears provide about the world around you. You will manage to get out of the cave and back into the light, even without being able to see where you're going, by using the information from your other sensory systems. Using all our senses, putting together the information from all of them, is how we survive.

But every one of us, by about the age of five or six, learns that one sensory system works better for us than the others do. We come to prefer that sensory system because we discover that it lets us take in more information, understand it better, remember it longer, and use it more efficiently. That system then becomes our *dominant* sensory system.

For the majority of people in the mainstream culture in today's United States of America, the preferred system is either sight or hearing. We don't know why. It may be that more people are born with eye or ear dominance; it may be that in our "Don't touch!" culture more of us *learn* to prefer our eyes or ears. Most likely, it's a combination of the two. Whatever the cause, the phenomenon is one we all know well. We can ask any teacher about the children in a class and get reports like these:

> "It makes no difference how many times you tell Jason how to do something. If you want him to do it right, you have to let him read about it, or watch a video, or look at some kind of picture or diagram."
>
> "Mary can look at information all day long . . . and she will eventually learn it. But she does a lot better if you simply

tell her what she needs to know or give her a tape to listen to."

"Frank just doesn't learn things by looking or listening; he really has trouble understanding information with his eyes and ears. But he could take any machine apart and put it back together perfectly, in the dark! What he needs is to get in there and deal with things hands-on."

Identifying Someone Else's Dominant Sensory System

We can find out which sensory system a person prefers the way that teachers and parents do . . . by observing the person's behavior over a long period of time. In older children and adults we can also find out—more quickly—by paying attention to the *language* that they use, especially when they are under stress.

Suppose you've suggested a plan to a man who works for you, and you've asked him for his opinion of your proposal. He knows you're human; like anyone else, you like to be told that your ideas are *good* ones. And you're his *boss.* In that situation he will be a little tense, because he knows he has to choose his words with care. And one of the choices he makes will probably tell you which is his dominant sensory system. Suppose you've made your suggestion and asked for his opinion; here are some possible answers he might give you:

1. "The way I see it, it's a good plan. It's clear, and I can see exactly how it would work. I like it."
2. "Your plan really sounds good to me—it rings all the right bells. I like it."
3. "I feel like your plan is exactly what we need. You've put your finger on all the right buttons. I like it."

Notice what happens? The first speaker's answer relies on words and phrases taken from the vocabulary of sight—"The way I see it" and "It's clear" and "I see how it would work." The second speaker uses more *ear* words and phrases—"Your plan sounds good" and "It rings all the right bells." And the third speaker leans heavily on the vocabulary of touch—"I feel like it's what we need" and "You've put your finger on the right buttons." These responses are typical in such situations. Because although people routinely use *all* the different sensory vocabularies in relaxed conversation and discussion, when they are tense and under stress they tend to choose the vocabulary that goes best with their dominant sensory system. This language behavior pattern is called a *sensory mode.*

Here are some possible *negative* responses to your request for a reaction to your plan:

1. *Sight Mode.* "It looks to me like your plan is maybe not as clear as it could be. I'm sorry; I don't see how it would work. Maybe you could shed a little more light on some of the blurry parts for me."

2. *Hearing Mode.* "It sounds to me as if there might be some problems with your plan; I'm sorry to have to say that. Maybe you could tell me a little more about it, just to get rid of some of the static for me."

3. *Touch Mode.* "I'm sorry; I don't think I get it. I can't put my finger on the exact problem, but something about your plan doesn't rub me the right way. Maybe you could go over it for me one more time and help me with the rough spots."

We all use these three sensory modes. We use others, too—we say "That whole project stinks," using smell mode; we say "What a sweet deal this is" or "The very idea leaves a bad taste in my mouth," in taste mode. We even mix up the modes and say things like "I see what you're saying." *In casual interactions, we use the vocabulary from all the sensory systems with ease.* This means that you don't decide someone is hearing dominant the first time you hear him say "That sounds terrific!" One or two examples of "I like the way it looks" or "Do you see what I mean?" don't mean that the speaker is sight dominant. But when you notice a pattern, when you notice words and phrases from the same sensory mode coming up again and again in someone's speech, you can safely conclude that the speaker prefers the sensory system that goes with that vocabulary.

In the mainstream American culture today, a preference for sight or hearing is encouraged. Sight is valued most of all, with hearing close behind. Not surprisingly, this creates problems for those who prefer touch, because that same culture actively discourages and disapproves of touch.

Identifying Your Own Dominant Sensory System

At this point you'll be wondering about your *own* sensory system preferences. If you haven't thought about them before, you may find it hard to decide which system is dominant for you. Ask yourself this question: How is it easiest for you to understand and learn and remember? Suppose you had to pack your own parachute and use it to jump out of an airplane. Which of the methods listed below would you rather use to get ready for that task? Which method strikes you as the one you would be *least* likely to use?

1. Read a set of instructions for packing parachutes and then watch a video on the subject.
2. Listen to a tape that gives clear and detailed instructions for packing parachutes, and then get an opportunity to ask questions about the subject and hear the answers.

3. Take several parachutes that are packed correctly and then unpack them to find out exactly how the packing is done.

Your answer to this problem (and to similar ones that you will find in the workout section for this chapter) will serve as a rough guide to the way you rank sight, hearing, and touch in your own interactions with the world. For me, the order of choice is #2, #3, and then #1; I am hearing dominant, with touch as my second preference and sight ranked last. You will find it useful to have that information for yourself and for anyone you are in frequent contact with.

The Problem with Being Touch Dominant

People I talk to about touch dominance today often seem to believe that our culture's current negative attitude toward touch is something absolutely natural and inevitable, something to be taken for granted. In fact, however, it's a relatively recent development. People used to do a great deal more touching than they do today, and it was not disapproved of. Even in the 1930s and 1940s, when I was a child, both men and women in a gathering picked children up and set them on their laps without the slightest hesitation. In the 1950s, camp counselors thought nothing of hugging and patting youngsters in their care. Friends and family members expected to be hugged and kissed when they arrived after even a short absence; kids held hands and played with one another's hair and clothing without any fear of being fussed at. Basically, touching was considered natural and wholesome.

And then there was a dramatic change. As the level of violence in our society began to rise, both in the real world and in the media, we began to interpret even the most casual sort of touching as either erotic behavior or potential physical violence. So that, for example, today's teachers and camp counselors and day care providers would not even *consider* touching children affectionately in the way that was entirely acceptable during the first half of the twentieth century. They know they would risk being charged with sexual abuse. Similarly, friends—perhaps especially friends who are of the same gender—are very careful about public touching, knowing that others are likely to take it as evidence of a sexual relationship. The exact level of tolerance differs from one area of the country to another, from one ethnic group to another, and within different families. But even in the most tolerant groups, there is a new wariness about touch, and a strong tendency to interpret any *unexplained* touch, as well as any touching from someone who's not a close friend or relative, negatively.

I understand the importance of protecting people from abusive touch, from unwelcome touch, and from touch as a demonstration of others' power. That goes without saying. What I want to emphasize here is that—given the *facts* about our current attitudes toward touch—touch dominant peoples' lives are being made complicated and difficult. Much more so than in even the recent past.

If you are in your forties or younger, your reaction as you were reading this section may very well have been, "Well, of course decent people disapprove of most touching! Everybody knows that!" In that case, please stay with me while we explore what that reaction may mean as you interact with people who perceive matters differently and who feel the same way about touch that you feel about sight or hearing.

What Can We Do to Help?

The obvious *easy* solution would be for touch dominant people simply to switch to a preference for sight or hearing; that would solve the entire problem at one fell swoop. Parents in my seminars often tell me they're going to go straight home and start switching their touch dominant children to one of the other senses. However, like many other obvious solutions, it seems to be almost impossible to carry out. To varying degrees, touch dominant people learn to cope and to substitute other senses for touch much of the time. But their preference does not change, and when they are under stress it can be overwhelming.

Suppose we go back to Scenario One and take another look at it. It was obvious that none of the people involved had any knowledge about the phenomenon of touch dominance or its implications for conversation. What if they *had* been well informed about it? How might things have gone differently? Could the Whitneys then have taken steps to avoid or repair the communication breakdown?

Another Look at Scenario One

If Mary and Frank Whitney had insisted on speaking Chinese throughout the scenario and Carolyn had insisted on speaking French, we'd know what to tell them to do. We'd tell them that either the child or the parents had to switch and speak the same language the others were speaking. The sensory modes aren't languages, but the principle is the same. Let's assume that the adult Whitneys, knowing that their daughter is touch dominant, voluntarily switched to touch language in the scenario. It might then have gone like this:

Mary: "Carolyn, I feel as if you should at least try to help me a little! You're not a baby, you're fifteen years old! Can't you understand that this is important?"

Carolyn: "Okay, Mom." (She goes on eating, without looking up.)

Frank: "Carolyn, it's hard for your mother to talk to you when you keep your head turned away from her like that."

Carolyn: "Oh, sure—I'm sorry." (She looks at her mother). "What do you want me to do, Mom?"

Mary: "Just one thing! Just take that card of paint chips and pick out one for your room. The painters will be here tomorrow; I've got to get this settled."

Carolyn: "But Mom—I really don't care how you paint it. No kidding, it just doesn't matter to me."

Mary: "Carolyn, I won't feel right about it unless you're the one who picks out the color. If you don't care, that won't be hard for you to do."

Carolyn: "You really want me to do that?"

Mary: "I really do."

Carolyn: "Okay, Mom. Sure. No problem."

This isn't perfect. It still seems to Mary and Frank that their daughter *should* be genuinely interested in the color choice for that paint. It still seems to Carolyn that a big fuss is being made over something trivial. But three things have changed dramatically for the better. First, Carolyn is going to choose a color, as her parents have asked her to do. Second, there was no communication breakdown. And third, nobody is angry.

The *people* in this scenario haven't changed; they are the same people they always were, with the same sensory preferences and the same personalities and attitudes they always had. They still disagree about the importance of color. *But their perceptions of one another are different.* Now Carolyn doesn't think of her parents as bullies; now Mary and Frank don't perceive their daughter as deliberately stubborn and contrary and uncooperative. Communication has taken place. This is a substantial improvement, and well worth the minor changes the parents had to make in their language to bring it about.

Workout Section One

✦

A Test To Help You Identify Your Preferred Sensory Mode

On some of the questions below you may find that *none* of the suggested answers is exactly right for you. When that happens, choose the one *closest* to something you would say or do in the situation described.

1. During a meeting, one of your partners claims that last year's profits were much lower than they should have been. You disagree. Which of the following would you be most likely to say?

   a. "That's not the way I see it."

   b. "That doesn't sound right to me."

   c. "That's not how I feel about it."

2. A friend is terribly discouraged and depressed, and convinced that a project is doomed because it's moving so slowly. You have faith in the project and in your friend. Which would you say?

   a. "Over the long term, this is sure to mean a bright future for you."

   b. "Over the long term, the results of this will be music to your ears."

   c. "Over the long term, this is going to make you feel like you're on top of the world."

3. You thought you were doing well in a project, but you've just been told that your efforts are disastrously bad. You disagree. Which would you say?

   a. "Look, you're not seeing the situation clearly."

b. "Listen, what I'm hearing from you is just plain wrong."

c. "I don't get it—I don't think you're in touch with the situation."

4. And suppose the person you're talking to in #3 says, "Really? Explain that to me, please." Which would you say?

   a. "Somebody has painted a picture for you that has no resemblance to reality!"

   b. "Somebody has told you a wild tale that's nothing but a garbled version of reality!"

   c. "Somebody who is completely out of touch with reality has really muddied the waters here."

5. You've just been elected president of an organization that really matters to you, when suddenly you're challenged from the floor. Someone stands up and says, "Wait, this is a terrible mistake!" Which would you say?

   a. "There's always room for another point of view."

   b. "There's always room for a song in a different key."

   c. "There's always room to put forward opposing ideas."

6. Suppose the boor described in #5 doesn't seem willing to give up and sit down. Which would you say?

   a. "My friend, I suggest you open your eyes: This election is over."

   b. "My friend, it doesn't sound to me as if you've been listening: This election is over."

   c. "My friend, I don't feel that you have a good grasp of the situation: This election is over."

7. One of your children has flatly refused to do an assigned chore and dared you to do something about it. Which would you say?

   a. "I *see!* It's quite clear—you've decided I'm the enemy and you've declared war!"

b. "I hear you loud and clear! You're telling me that I'm the enemy—and you've declared war!"

c. "Let me get this straight! You feel like I'm the enemy—and you've declared war!"

8. You're alone in the middle of a swamp, facing what you believe to be aliens from outer space. You want to give them a message that you're an intelligent creature with friendly intentions. Which would you do?

   a. Draw a picture in the mud with a stick.

   b. Sing the most complicated song you know, loudly.

   c. Make a figure out of mud and sticks.

9. You and your spouse have had a serious disagreement. You're sorry, but you're not willing to change your mind. Which would you say?

   a. "Please—try to see things my way, just this once."

   b. "Please—try to speak my language, just this once."

   c. "Please—try to go along with my feelings, just this once."

10. You have been selected to decide what will appear on a new United States one-dollar coin. Which would you choose?

    a. A picture of your favorite tree.

    b. Your favorite brief proverb or saying.

    c. A deeply carved and textured border around the edge of the coin.

11. Your doctor has ordered you to join a club for relaxation and recreation. Which would you choose?

    a. A colored-pencil sketching club.

    b. A barbershop quartet club.

    c. A woodcarving group.

12. You're at a restaurant with good friends and good food—but you're leaving. Which of the following would be most likely to cause you to do that?

    a. There's a large fish on the plate next to you, with its head still on and one eye staring up at you.

    b. The sound system keeps playing one song—a song you don't even like—over and over.

    c. The chair you're sitting on is so hard and so straight that you're not comfortable.

13. You have to give a short talk for your local chamber of commerce. Which of these topics would you pick?

    a. How the Future Looks to Me.

    b. The Sweet Sound of Success.

    c. A Strong Hand at the Helm.

14. You've decided to do something substantial for your alma mater, and you can afford to. Which would you donate?

    a. An original oil painting in a handsome frame.

    b. A pipe organ for the college auditorium.

    c. A large bronze sculpture for the quad.

15. You've met someone you think might turn out to be part of a romantic relationship, and you want to say so—but not too abruptly. Which would you say?

    a. "When two people see the world the same way . . ."

    b. "When two people sing the same song . . ."

    c. "When two people just seem to go together perfectly . . ."

All A answers are sight mode; all B answers are hearing mode; all C answers are touch mode. Count up your answers in each mode to find out which you prefer.

Your answers to the above problems (and to similar ones that you will find in the following workout section) will serve as a rough guide to the way you rank sight, hearing, and touch in your own interactions with the world.

Touchpoints

1. "Ironically, touch is one of the first systems to develop in the human . . . yet the last sensory system to be given attention. There are institutes for the study of all the other senses but none for touch, and too few researchers are working on touch."*

   (Nina Gunzenhauser, editor, "Appendix: Research Issues and Direction," pp. 163–167 in *Advances in Touch: New Implications in Human Development*, Johnson & Johnson 1990; p. 163.)

2. "The communications we transmit through touch constitute the most powerful means of establishing human relationships, the foundation of experience."

   (Ashley Montagu, *Touching: The Human Significance of the Skin*, third edition, Harper & Row 1986; p. xv.)

3. "Every other sense has a key organ to study; for touch that organ is the skin, and it stretches over the whole body."

   (Diane Ackerman, *A Natural History of the Senses*, Random House 1990, p. 77.)

4. "Look at what we ask of the skin. We take for granted that it will carry out its function as a barrier against a host of dangers. We count on it as a major enhancer of our attractiveness. But as the skin does these things for us—while, incidentally, remaking itself every 28 days or so—it is at the same time coordinating and orchestrating on our behalf an incredibly complex array of activities."

   (Richard Edelson, quoted in "More Than Skin Deep," by Albert Rosenfield, *Science Illustrated*, August/September 1988, pp. 15–17; on p. 17.)

*This situation has improved somewhat. Very active research on touch is now going on under the direction of Dr. Tiffany Fields at the Touch Research Institute (TRI), University of Miami School of Medicine, PO Box 016820, Miami FL 33101. TRI publishes a newsletter (called *Touchpoints*) and offers training workshops.

Talking Touch

1. Some touch words that were once in common use in English, but are now obsolete:

felth	the power of feeling in the fingers (and other parts of the skin); like sight and hearing
hardel	the back of the hand, as "palm" is the other side of the hand
wrine	a deep line in the face; a "wrinkle" is a shallow wrine
yespen	a double handful; as much as two hands can hold
handfast	a contract sealed by clasping hands
feelsome	a word describing something that is a pleasure to touch; velvet would be "feelsome"
lithesome	flexible
handsmooth	flat and level
to chumble	to crumble something into tiny bits
to twingle	to twine around

2. And here are some touch language items that aren't obsolete, but that would be found only in medical or technical writing:

knismable	ticklish
knismogenic	producing a tickling sensation
anaphia	lost (or diminished) sense of touch
palpatc	to examine by touching

skinfeel	a term used by experts on product standards; for example, for hand lotions and shampoos
thigmoreceptor	receptor cell for external touch
proprioceptor	receptor cell for internal touch

3. Many sets of English words for sensory experience have words for sight and hearing but no word for *touch*; some examples follow. I suggest setting up a file for sets like these (in a notebook or on your computer). In that way, when you come across more examples, you can add them to your touch dominance database; and if you suddenly find one of the missing pieces, it will be handy for you to fill in the blank. (Note: If you're willing to share your discoveries, the information would be welcomed by the Touch Dominance Network, which is at P.O. Box 1137, Huntsville, Arkansas 72740-1137. Please send them along; the Network will send you an information packet in exchange.)

   a. "I didn't just see it by accident—I was looking."
   "I didn't just hear it by accident—I was listening."
   "I didn't just touch it by accident—I was ______ ."
   "I didn't just feel it by accident—I was ______ ."

   b. "Look at me when I talk to you!"
   "Listen to me when I talk to you!"
   "______ when I talk to you!"

   c. "You're the apple of my eye!"
   "You're music to my ears!"
   "You're ______ to my skin!"

   d. "Mary's nearsighted; Ann's vision-impaired; Tom's blind."

"Mary's hard of hearing; Ann's hearing-impaired; Tom's deaf."
"Mary's ______ ; Ann's touch-impaired (?); Tom's ______ ."

e. "The image we saw was perfectly clear."
"The sound we heard was perfectly clear."
"The texture we touched/felt was ______ ."

Chapter Two

Growing Up with Rough Edges—The Touch Dominant Child

Scenario Two

"How do you do that, Gary?" Bobby asked. "How does it work? Hey, I want to play, too!"

Gary looked up from the electronic game he was holding in his hands and grinned at the other boy. "It's easy," he said. "I'll show you how. Watch me!" The lights on the little game flashed brightly and it beeped twice before its mechanical voice announced Gary's score. "Okay? See, you push the red one and then the green one and then you look at the stuff on the screen to see what you're supposed to do next. Okay? Now it's <u>your</u> turn!" He held the toy out to Bobby. "Here!"

"But I don't know how to <u>do</u> it," Bobby objected. He didn't reach for the game; instead, he put both hands behind him and moved back a couple of steps.

"Huh?" Still offering the game, Gary made an exasperated face. "I just <u>showed</u> you, dummy!" he said sharply. "Didn't you see me?"

"I guess so." Billy's voice was low and sullen, and he stared down at the ground.

"Well, then! You said you wanted a turn!"

"I don't remember what you did," said Billy miserably. "You did it too fast!" He looked up quickly, not quite meeting the other boy's eyes. "Do it for me again, okay?"

"Look," Gary said, almost yelling now, "I showed you twice yesterday, and you acted like you're acting now! You're just scared to try, you chicken!"

"No, I'm not. I'm not chicken! Give me one more chance, Gary, okay?"

"No! I don't want to! Go play with somebody else!"

From the front window of the house, Susan watched the familiar scene with a heavy heart; it seemed to her that it happened almost every time anybody came over to play with Bobby. Whether the kids ended up rolling around on the ground fighting or the other child just yelled at Bobby and then walked away, as Gary was doing now, Bobby was almost always left alone and in tears. He didn't seem to have *any* idea how to get along with other children.

Susan was both baffled and worried; she had hoped things would get better as Bobby grew older, but he was ten now and there was no sign of any change. How was her son going to manage in life, she wondered, if he couldn't learn even the most basic social skills?

✦

What's Going on Here?

Most children can learn to play a simple game by using their eyes and their ears. From Gary's point of view, he's given Bobby plenty of information: Push the red button, then the green one, and then look at the words on the screen that will tell the player what to do from there. He's told Bobby, and he's shown him, twice on the previous day and again today. The way Gary sees it, it's so simple a baby could do it, and

Bobby's just wasting their playtime on purpose, the way he always does.

Unfortunately, Bobby has a very hard time remembering what he sees and hears, especially when he's already scared that he's making a fool of himself in front of another child. He hears the words Gary is saying, but they don't stay with him; he saw what Gary was doing with the buttons, but the sequence was so fast that he couldn't keep track of it. He knows the game is an expensive toy, and he's scared he'll break it if he does it wrong. If Gary would just go a little *slower*, he thinks, he could get it, but he *always* does stuff too fast! In Bobby's opinion, Gary's just showing off to make him feel stupid, the way he always does.

This is going to happen over and over again in Bobby's life unless something is done to help him. Every time it happens, he'll grow a little bit more certain that there's something very wrong with him, and that other people are *right* to reject him. And that conviction will be enough to send him into every human interaction already tense and nervous, braced for yet another social failure, and expecting the worst. It's no wonder his mother is worried about him; she *should* be worried.

What Life Is Like for the Touch Dominant Child

Touch dominant children go through their lives, much of the time, as if they had to do everything while wearing heavy mittens on both hands. They have the kinds of days and nights that sight or hearing dominant kids would have if they had to do everything with something blocking their use of their eyes or ears.

The tools our culture uses to help children grow up to be happy and successful adults strongly favor eyes and ears. A very large part of the touch dominant child's time is spent doing the things on the following list:

- Listening to parents and teachers and "in charge" adults of all kinds, most of whom will not be using the touch vocabulary as they talk.
- Reading books and other publications.
- Looking at maps and charts and illustrations.
- Watching television and films.
- Participating in language interaction—conversations and interviews and the like—in sight mode and hearing mode, both with adults and with other children.

Touch dominant children can do all these things, but they have to work harder at them than sight and hearing dominant children do. When conditions are very good and they're given a level playing field, they manage very well. But much of the time conditions are anything *but* good.

Parents in the United States today are too busy and too tired (and often too worried) to spend much time with their children or give them full and careful attention. Teachers have too many children in their classrooms, and are coping with too wide a variety of problems. They have to deal with multilingual and multicultural classrooms, budget shortages, labor crises, guns and drugs and AIDS, for example. They're in no position to provide the extra help that's needed. Families are so scattered that touch dominant kids are often far away from the grandparents and aunts and uncles who filled "parenting" gaps in the past; often these children are latchkey kids, going home to no company but the television and the radio. Often they don't have many friends, either, because they don't get along well with the sight and hearing dominant children who make up most of their peer group. It's not surprising that they so frequently run into trouble.

Let's look at two dialogues that are typical of the touch dominant child's language environment. (You saw a shorter version of Dialogue Three earlier in the book.)

DIALOGUE THREE—A TEACHER AND A CHILD

Child: "I need some help—I don't get this!"

Teacher: "That's because you aren't even *looking* at it! It's not written on the ceiling, Sharon! How do you *expect* to learn anything if you can't even *see* it? It's right there on the page in front of your eyes—just *look* at it!"

Child: "But I don't *get* it! It's too *hard*."

Teacher: "I see no reason why you should be having trouble with it, Sharon—except that you're not trying."

Child: "I *am* trying! I just don't *get* it, *that's* all!"

Teacher: "Look, I don't have time for this nonsense. You look at your worksheet again, carefully, and I don't want to see you staring out the window or up at the ceiling. Keep your eyes on your work and try again."

Child: "It's no use. I can't do it. I'll never be able to do it."

Teacher: "Now, *see here*! There are twenty-four other children in this class who have to finish this page too! How are they supposed to work if you keep disturbing the class? Do you think you're being fair to them, acting this way?"

Child: (MISERABLE SILENCE.)

Teacher: "Well, Sharon?"

Child: "I don't know. I'm *sorry*!"

I'm sure you'll have no trouble imagining a version of the preceding dialogue in which the speakers are a child and a parent trying to help with the homework—or a version in which the worksheet is a test, making the stress on the child even worse.

DIALOGUE FOUR—A PARENT AND A CHILD

Parent: "Will you please explain to me why you are always so dirty when you come home from school? How does that happen?"

Child: "Just doing stuff."

Parent: "Like what?"

Child: "I don't know . . . just stuff."

Parent: "I work too hard to buy decent clothes for you to let you ruin them 'doing stuff'! Will you please sit down and read a book, or watch television or something, and stay out of trouble?"

Child: "But I don't want to!"

Parent: "And I don't want to see you looking like a pigpen again! Is that clear?"

Child: (LONG SIGH; LONG FACE.)

It will be obvious to you that touch dominant children like those in the scenarios and dialogues have to cope with a variety of different sources of trouble *all at the same time.* It's not just other kids, or just the teacher, or just their parents—it's all of them, and often other people as well. These children will tell you very clearly what *they* believe is going on. "I'm always in trouble," they'll say. "I can't do anything right. Nobody likes me!" And if they're as old as nine or ten, they'll add, "And I don't blame them."

They're only children, and they have to face all this without the benefit of any explanation. They don't know what's wrong, and everyone they try to communicate with leaps to the conclusion that the source of the trouble is some flaw in their character. Children who don't know how to explain and who are constantly being given messages like "You're not trying" and "You're just being difficult" and "You always spoil things for everybody else" and "You just don't care" eventually begin to believe that all those negative judgments must be true. After all, everybody seems to agree and nobody has any *positive* suggestions to make! How could the whole adult world, not to mention all the other kids, be wrong? Pretty soon, most of these children *do* stop trying, because it seems obvious to them that it's hopeless.

It doesn't have to be like this. We can't change the world to make touch more acceptable, but we can *help.* Let's rewrite those two dialogues.

DIALOGUE THREE, REVISED

Child: "I need some help—I don't get this!"

Teacher: "I feel sure you can do it, Sharon."

Child: "Will you help me? Please?"

Teacher: "Sure I will. Put your finger on the part that's hardest for you, so I'll know where the trouble is."

Child: "Right here . . . [puts her finger on the page] . . . where it starts about pioneers. . . . I don't get it."

Teacher: "You're supposed to finish the sentence that starts with 'When the pioneers had to cross the desert in their covered wagons, their worst fear was . . .' And what would you put down next?"

Child: "I don't know."

Teacher: "Think about it a minute. How would you feel if you had to do that? What would you feel scared about?"

Child: "Oh! I can do it!"

Teacher: "I knew you could. Now, try to work quietly so the rest of the class can get the page done, too, please."

This is the same worried child, and the same busy teacher, but the two are communicating without fighting. Much of Sharon's problem is fear; she has little confidence in her ability to deal with information just by looking at it and she has had many past experiences that reinforce her lack of confidence. She knows the answer to the question, but her nervousness about this type of task is interfering with her ability to do the work. The teacher does several useful things here. Switching to touch mode instead of lecturing in sight mode about looking at the page helps tremendously, as does offering the child reassurance instead of criticism. And reading the problem sentence aloud helps Sharon, too, by providing the information in a second sensory format. It takes no more of the teacher's time to do it this way, but the outcome is very different.

DIALOGUE FOUR, REVISED

Parent: "Will you please explain to me how you get so dirty on your way home from school? How does that happen?"

Child: "Just doing stuff."

Parent: "What kind of stuff gets you so dirty? I don't understand. Do you dig tunnels and crawl through them?"

Child: "No Dad. I think it's maybe from climbing trees."

Parent: "That would do it. And I know that's fun for you."

Child: "Am I not supposed to?"

Parent: "Not when you've got your good clothes on, son—think about it. They cost a lot of money, and I have to work hard to buy them."

Child: "I'm sorry. I'll be more careful, okay? I'll put on my play clothes first."

Parent: "Good idea. That would help a lot."

Notice that this father doesn't have to soften the message he wants to get across to his son: that he has to be more careful with his school clothes, which parents have to work hard to earn money for. Switching to touch mode *to help the child communicate more effectively* doesn't require the adult to cater to the boy or to sacrifice any adult needs or principles. But when both adult and child are speaking the same language, misunderstandings are much less likely.

The changes I've shown in the rewritten dialogues are dramatic; it may not be that easy. If the child has had a long experience of always being in the wrong and has built up a strong expectation that nothing will ever be any better, adults who try using touch mode to improve communication should be prepared for it to *take* a little while. The younger the child is, the lower the barriers already in place will be. But even when the first few tries are met with nothing but "I don't get it" and "I don't know" and "Sorry" and sullen silence, adults who stick with it will begin to see positive effects.

The Necessity of Touch for Normal Development

We know that touch is critical for the normal development of children. Most parents today have read about the research in which hospitalized infants who were given more touching gained more weight and strength than other infants who didn't receive that extra stimulus. Few parents now believe that it spoils babies to pick them up when they cry, or to rock them and cuddle them. On the contrary! Today we see babies everywhere being carried about in Snuglis by both mothers and fathers. Similarly, most parents will let infants and toddlers handle things pretty freely as long as there is no danger to either the child or what's being handled.

But there is a strong tendency for even very well-informed parents to draw a line suddenly when a child is about four and announce that the time for touching is over. For eye and ear dominant children, this may be a trivial matter, but for touch dominant children it's anything but trivial.

The Problems of Touch Dominant Children

In Chapter Four we'll take up the question of what adults and older kids can do to make the transition into a "Don't touch!" world easier. For now, however, let's summarize the problems that touch dominant children have to deal with.

FIRST: Almost everything they're required to do is a little harder for them than it is for the eye and ear kids. Not because they're any less intelligent or competent, but because our society is so biased in favor of sight and hearing. (The exception is, of course, activities like athletics, where a preference for touch is allowed and may even be rewarded. But not all touch dominant kids are fond of sports, and even those who are have to spend most of their time doing other things.)

SECOND: Because TD kids tend to be slow getting eye and ear things done, people (including other children) get irritated with them. This leads to tension and stress, which makes the touch dominant child even more likely to rely on touch mode and even less able to use sight and hearing efficiently.

THIRD: The everyday English vocabulary for touch mode is more limited than for sight and hearing mode, and is often perceived as somehow inferior to those other modes. There's no logical reason why "I see" should be considered more intelligent and sophisticated than "I get it"; it's a matter of fashion. But touch dominant children, already carrying a heavy load because everything around them favors the eye and the ear, often have the additional burden of not being able to find effective words for what they want to say.

Notice, for example, that I can talk about "eye kids" and "ear kids," or about "eye and ear things," but English has no equivalent touch mode phrases. If I tried to use "skin kids" or "flesh things" in the same way, I'd be in trouble! In the past we had the English word "felth"; we could say "He has excellent felth," just as we can now say "She has excellent sight" or "He has very good hearing." Unfortunately, that useful word has long since been dropped from our language, along with many others that would be welcomed in the touch vocabulary. This language shortfall comes up constantly in the lives of touch dominant children.

FOURTH: Because touch is so important to these children, they naturally are more *likely* to touch, and to rely more heavily on "body language," than are sight and hearing dominant children. The more tense they are, the more worried and frustrated and upset, the more likely they are to try to communicate with their bodies instead of with words. Especially when they find themselves "at a loss for words" because there don't seem to be any that will *work*. In our culture this leads to difficulties. Children who touch others, unless the touching has been requested and is from a set of *approved* kinds of touching, *get in trouble*. That's just the way it is. We associate touching with sex and violence, and we come down hard on children who try it.

Not surprisingly, these children have a hard time of it. They're trying to get along in the world and do everything that's expected of them—already hard enough, without anything extra laid on—and then they're handed these four additional burdens to carry. Worst of all, they usually don't understand *why*. Like everyone else around them, they're baffled. They just know that "I'm always in trouble" and "Everything I do is wrong" and "Nobody likes me." They run into one rejection after another, and—because they're human—they grow more and more "rejectable" as they go along. If you don't expect anybody to like you, you stop trying to be likable; that's only natural.

Along the way, people who interact with touch dominant children stick labels on them, and write those labels into the files that now go with us from birth to death. Sometimes these labels are the fancy kind: "dyslexic, slow learner, underachiever, hyperactive, withdrawn." I'm not suggesting that there aren't many valid examples of children so labeled, only that touch dominant children may sometimes get these labels by mistake. And the touch dominant child who is accurately diagnosed with one of these other conditions has *extra* problems. Sometimes the labels are simpler: "stupid, slow, hostile, uncooperative, lazy . . . *bad.*"

Whether labels are fancy or simple, they're terribly hard to get rid of, once attached. Everything the child does tends to be interpreted in terms of the label. This is especially bad when, as often happens, the person doing the interpreting sees the label before seeing the child; the labels create expectations in advance. And by the time touch dominant people are into their teens, they have usually accepted the labels and believe them. Convincing these youngsters that they're *not* stupid, or bad—or worse—often becomes almost impossible.

This is a sorry state of affairs, and needs fixing. For most touch dominant children, life can be a very rough row to hoe.

Another Look at Scenario Two

Let's go back to the scenario that was at the beginning of this chapter and go over it one more time. Unlike the example dialogues, the scenario showed a touch dominant child involved in a communication breakdown with *another* child, one of his peers. Our children aren't likely to know how to switch to a different sensory mode to accommodate a playmate. We've never taught them that technique, or even the principles on which it's based.

Parents (and other adults) need to realize that touch dominant (TD) children, most of the time, will have to interact with sight and hearing peers. Because the other children will find that situation perfectly satisfactory, it's the touch dominant child who will have to learn a strategy for improving the interactions. Let's assume that Bobby has done that; how might Scenario Two have gone differently?

Bobby: "How do you do that, Gary? How does it work? Hey, I want to play, too!"

Gary: "It's easy. I'll show you how. Watch me!"

Bobby: "Wait a minute—can I hold it while you show me?"

Gary: "Sure." (Hands Bobby the toy.) "Now, first you push the red one and then . . . what's the matter?"

Bobby: "I need for you to go slow enough so I can do it while you're telling me, okay?"

Gary: "Oh . . . okay. First, push that red thing there."

Bobby: "Got it. Now what?"

Gary: "Now push the green one . . . right! . . . Now you look at the words that you see on the screen, okay? That tells you what to do next."

Bobby: "Okay! Got it!"

Same two boys; same problem. But a substantially different, and more positive, outcome.

Workout Section Two

✦

1. A sight dominant child can use a sight metaphor—"I'm a flower!" or "I'm a star!" A hearing dominant child can say, "I'm a bell!" or "I'm a drum!" But what about touch dominant children? Can you think of touch metaphors that they can use?

2. Touch dominant youngsters need to learn—in advance—some explanations of their problem, so that when they have to explain they won't be tongue-tied. (Like the child in the revised Scenario Two, who knew to tell his friend, "I need to hold it while you show me.") Here are two possibilities; try to add a few more.

   - "When things are hard for me, I have to stop and get in touch with the problem before I try to do anything else."

   - "Sometimes it's hard for me to understand a problem when I'm too close to it. To grasp it properly I have to move back and give myself some room. Nobody can see a tree with their eyes flat against its trunk."

3. These sentences are commonly used when speaking to children. Can you think of touch equivalents for them, to use with a TD child? If not, does it matter?

   - "I don't see why you can't follow instructions!"
   - "Keep your eyes on your work!"
   - "It's clear to me that you're not trying."
   - "You look [or sound] worried."
   - "See if you can make your answer more clear."
   - "Watch what you're doing, please!"

- "The look on your face worries me; are you okay?" (Or "The way your voice sounds . . .")

4. On pages 165–168 at the end of this book, you'll find a touch language "translation" of "Goldilocks and the Three Bears" (titled "Curlylocks and the Three Bears") to read to a touch dominant child. You might want to try your hand at doing the same thing for another children's story or two. ("The Princess and the Pea" is a good choice for TD children just as it is, of course.)

Touchpoints

1. "Touch is a means of communication so critical that its absence retards growth in infants. . . . The new research suggests that certain brain chemicals released by touch, or others released in its absence, may account for these infants' failure to thrive."

(Daniel Goleman, "The Experience of Touch: Research Points to a Critical Role," *The New York Times*, February 2, 1988.)

2. "We must ask, 'Why isn't the material reaching the student?' rather than 'Why isn't the student grasping the material?' "

(Barbara Meister Vitale, *Unicorns Are Real: A Right-Brained Approach to Learning*, Jalmar Press 1982; on p. vii. This book is not specifically about teaching touch dominant children, but it has many excellent suggestions for doing so.)

3. "Last year hyperactive 9-year-old Javier . . . seemed unable to concentrate on anything long enough to complete simple assignments in school. . . . Young Javier was classified as a kinesthetic learner—one who learns best by manipulating objects. So teacher Rosenthal set him to work with a set of Lego-like blocks that join and separate to represent arithmetic equations. The boy suddenly discovered he enjoyed mathematics."

(William Tucker, "Foot in the Door," *Forbes*, February 3, 1992, pp. 50–52; on p. 50. This article reports on an education firm that divides children into "visual," "audio," and "kinesthetic" learners—that is, into sight, hearing, and touch dominant learners—and trains teachers to make good use of that information. Many sources divide touch dominant children into "tactile" or "tactual," which refers to handling and touching, and "kinesthetic," which refers to position and balance of the body.)

4. "I was a terrible student. I couldn't take that stuff off of the page and get it into my head."

(Tom Watson of IBM, quoted in "Adventures (and Misadventures) of Watson Fellows," by Ted Gup, pp. 68–80, *Smithsonian Magazine,* September 1994; on p. 78. This is the best statement of the learning difficulties of touch dominant students as *they* perceive them that I've ever come across anywhere; you might add it to the list for #2 on page 36.)

5. "Some children have what we call sensitive skin, in the same way that other children have sensitive palates or don't like bright lights. For that child, a brief hug is equivalent to a 10-minute cuddle with another child."

(Stanley Turecki, child psychiatrist, quoted in "Knowing When to Touch," by Lawrence Kutner, *The New York Times,* June 29, 1989.)

6. "Studies of infants and children have shown that nothing is more important to early physical and mental growth than touch."

(Kathryn Barnett, "A Theoretical Construct of the Concepts of Touch As They Relate to Nursing," *Nursing Research,* March/April 1972, pp. 102–110; on p. 104.)

Talking Touch

1. When you communicate, you may . . .

get in touch	stay in touch
make contact	touch bases
ask sharp questions	get right to the point
touch a nerve	throw out an idea
twist what was said	give somebody strokes
stand up to somebody	get something off your chest
put yourself forward	hang back
hang in there	feel completely out of it
put the pressure on	make a point
touch on a subject	point out a fact
cling to an idea	press for a decision
put out a feeler	hold your own
stand your ground	hold that thought

2. When you're unhappy . . .

life is rough	things are tough
it breaks your heart	it's like a slap in the face
you feel really down	you're down in the dumps
you feel really low	it's a heavy load to carry
it's hard to bear	you need something to hold on to
you feel crushed	your heart sinks

Chapter Three

Between a Rock and a Hard Place—The Touch Dominant Adult

Scenario Three

Jim Drake looked up from his newspaper as Melanie came into the room.

"Hi, honey!" he said. "You look worn out—is everything okay?"

"Oh, sure!" she answered, sitting down on the couch across from him. She leaned back and closed her eyes, taking a long deep breath. "It's just the traffic out there! I thought I was never going to get home."

"Well, I'm glad you're here. How did Mom look?"

Melanie opened her eyes and smiled at him. "Jim, I feel so much better about her now. She was sitting up in bed and she had me fix her pillows half a dozen times and—"

"But how did she look?" Jim insisted. "When I saw her yesterday she was white as a sheet, and you could tell from her eyes that she was hurting. Come on, honey—did she look better this afternoon?"

Melanie cleared her throat. "Well," she said slowly, "I don't really know. I was just so glad she felt stronger and could move around better; I guess I didn't think about anything else."

"Well, was she wearing the new robe we gave her?"

Melanie looked down at her hands. "I don't know, Jim," she said. "I'm sorry."

"But you were just there! You mean you just spent a whole hour with my mother and you don't even know what she was wearing?" Jim smacked the newspaper against the arm of his chair. "Melanie, that's ridiculous!"

Her lips tightened; when she answered him, her voice was cold. "Maybe you'd better go visit your mother yourself from now on, Jim," she said.

"You knew I'd want to know how she looked!" he said angrily. "Anybody would! I don't see why I can't trust you for even the simplest little things!"

She looked straight at him then. "Remember me?" she said bitterly. "I'm the stupid one in the family! Remember?"

✦

What's Going on Here?

In Scenario Three we see a couple who genuinely love one another, but who are communicating very badly. Melanie Drake is touch dominant and has little or no interest in the *looks* of things. She's very fond of Jim's mother and has been worried about her, and the hospital setting was anything but relaxed; this combination of stressful factors was enough to lock all her conscious attention into her own preferred sensory system. She literally has no conscious memory of the visual details of her visit with Mrs. Drake. Jim, on the other hand, is sight dominant, and it seems impossible to him that she could have spent any length of time with his mother without noticing at least the basic information about her appearance. His own worried state makes that information even more important to him than it would ordinarily be.

From Melanie's point of view, she has just spent a difficult couple of hours demonstrating her love and concern for her family, not to mention battling heavy traffic at the end of a long day, only to have Jim show no appreciation at all for her efforts. As usual, he has picked out some trivial little detail and started a fight over it. It seems to her that there's no pleasing him, no matter how hard she tries.

From Jim's point of view, if Melanie was paying so little attention to his mother that she can't even remember what the sick woman was wearing, she might as well not have gone. It seems to him that she was only going through the motions and didn't really care about his mother's condition or about his feelings. As usual, she can't be bothered to do anything more than halfway right, even when it's something that really matters.

Each of these people is baffled and hurt by the other's behavior and by the fact that these things seem to happen all the time—*especially* when it really matters. The communication breakdowns that are caused by sensory mode conflict don't happen when people are relaxed and unconcerned. Jim knows Melanie tends not to pay attention to visual things; Melanie knows very well that it's the visual details that matter to Jim. They've been married a long time. In a casual situation, they would both remember how they differ in this regard and would work around it. It's only in tense circumstances—which is, unfortunately, when they most *need* to be able to communicate well—that the system fails them.

For Jim, the argument is just another demonstration of Melanie's lack of care and concern; for Melanie, it's just one more demonstration that she's "the stupid one in the family" and might as well give up.

Why? Why do these two sensible, intelligent adults, who love one another and are doing their best to get along together, keep falling into foolish arguments like the one in this scenario? To find the answer, let's turn to the question of . . .

What Life Is Like for the Touch Dominant Adult

We live in a society where the most important question adults have to answer is this one: "What do you do?" That is, what is your profession? Your role in life?

A few touch dominant adults find themselves in fields where touch dominance is an asset, such as surgery, sculpture, professional dancing, or contact sports. Or in one of the skilled trades (auto mechanics, carpentry, stonemasonry) or skilled crafts (pottery, weaving, wood carving). For them, although their money and status varies, there is satisfaction in their work, and the pleasure of easy communication with other surgeons and dancers and mechanics. These are the lucky ones.

Many others have to spend their days working in fields where touch dominance is a handicap, fields where you can do well only by relying on your eyes and/or your ears. This is true for most of the prestigious professions—for lawyers, for most doctors, for most college professors, for architects and interior designers, for psychiatrists . . . the list is a long one. It's true for most teachers at every level; teaching is usually an eye/ear job. It's true for clerical and support staff. And many jobs for which sensory dominance isn't relevant, such as working the counter at a fast-food restaurant, offer only low pay and low status.

As for the difficult and important task of looking after a home and family, which is Melanie Drake's job, our society gives so little value to that role that we don't pay homemakers at *all.* We say a lot of nice things about the homemaker (who is still almost always a woman) and we go all out for Mother's Day. But the phrase "only a housewife"—plus the bald fact that the monetary value of homemakers' labor isn't even included when we compute such statistics as the gross national product—makes matters quite clear. Housekeeping, tending children and the elderly, practical nursing, all are roles for which touch is extremely important. All of them are low-pay (or no-pay), low-status roles.

To make things worse, a large percentage of touch dominant adults are unpopular. If they're surgeons, like the impossibly difficult Mark Craig on television's *St. Elsewhere,* they will get all sorts of rewards in the shape of high salaries and the perks and status that go with high salaries—*but people won't like them.* This matters. Being disliked is easier to bear when you're a high-paid surgeon than when you're an auto mechanic just barely making ends meet, but it always hurts. When you must handle constant rejection *without* money and status to smooth things over, the pain cuts even deeper.

Touch dominant adults, like touch dominant children, must get by in a society in which the method for processing information that serves them best is, much of the time, against the rules. Often they have built solid coping skills and they've found ways to compensate and balance things out. As long as their lives go smoothly, they do well. When they are under stress, however—and much of life in the United States today is almost by definition highly stressful—their coping skills are likely to desert them. Furthermore, decades of negative experience can make the TD adult touchy, quick to assume the worst, and hard to get along with, even when the stress is trivial. As in Dialogue Five, where a touch dominant man is trying to communicate with two hearing dominant colleagues:

DIALOGUE FIVE

Man: "Can I join you two ladies for lunch?"

Woman 1: "Well . . . we've been trying all morning long to find some time to talk about the new project."

Man: "Great! I've got some ideas about that project that I'd like to bounce around a while myself!"

Woman 2: "That sounds interesting. But listen, Maria and I really need to discuss this by ourselves. There are all kinds of things we have to talk over in words of one syllable. You'd really be bored."

Man: "Oh, I get it! You don't want me bothering you. FINE! Just pretend I'm not in the room, okay?"

Woman 1: "There you go again, turning anything anybody says to you into an insult! It's always the same old story with you, Carl, isn't it?"

Man: "Hey . . . I didn't just fall off the tree, you know! You don't want me around? That's fine with me! I'll get out of your hair!"

Carl could be right, of course; it could be that these two women don't like him, don't want his company, and are just trying to get rid of him. But he may be wrong. The problem is that *he will jump to that conclusion at the slightest sign of anything less than an enthusiastic welcome with open arms.*

The result is that when people who don't feel that way about him at all tell him the simple truth—for example, that they have to talk about something they're sure he would find boring, and they can't postpone it—it's very hard for them to make him understand or believe them. If they're like most adults in our society—busy and overburdened—they may not feel inclined to make the effort, especially when it keeps happening over and over again. It's easier just to say, after he has gone away hurt and angry, "Oh, well . . . nobody can get along with Carl; it's a waste of time to try. I gave up on that a long time ago."

Touch dominant adults' lives consist of one self-fulfilling prophecy after another. They *expect* to be rejected by other people. When they approach others they are so braced for a negative response that almost anything said to them gets a negative interpretation. This is exactly what they *thought* would happen, and it confirms their expectations. Other people sense their tension and uneasiness and react to it with tension of their own, which also interferes with the chances for successful communication.

This phenomenon feeds on itself, and it gets worse and worse as the years go by. So much so that it can be very difficult to turn the situation around unless everyone involved is patient and determined and deeply committed. Even if the two women in Dialogue Five had tried to use touch language with Carl, it might not have been possible for them to avoid hurting his feelings. If he is already deeply convinced that no one wants him around, he may misunderstand in spite of their best efforts. And once again they will say that it's a waste of time to try. This is why it's so important to begin dealing with the problem as early in life as possible.

Touch Dominance and Sexual Gender

It's important to realize that things would be no different if the speakers in the dialogue were a touch dominant woman and two male colleagues, instead of the other way around. You can go back to Dialogue Five and switch the genders in every line; you'll see that nothing else changes.

The touch dominant man's behavior is somewhat more likely to be mistaken for a sexual overture or potential violence than that of a touch dominant woman, simply because most men are larger and seem more threatening than most women. But the difference is a slim one, and growing slimmer every day, especially in interactions between adults and children. And when—as in Dialogue Five—the encounter includes no language that could possibly be perceived as erotic or violent, gender is largely irrelevant.

How Do Touch Dominant People Manage?

Many touch dominant adults do establish strong and solid relationships with other people, especially when they have skills that are highly valued and that make it worthwhile to tolerate their clumsy social behavior. The relationships may get off to a rocky start, but over time, others who know them well realize that their usual way of communicating doesn't accurately express their feelings and ideas. These other people may then try hard to help by acting as a kind of personal *translator.* You hear them making comments like these:

- "Don't pay attention to the way he talks—it's just his manner. He's not really like that at all."
- "I want you to know . . . she's really a kind and caring person. Just ignore the things she says."
- "When you get to know him, you'll realize that he is one of the most brilliant people we've ever had working here. I know it's hard to believe when you listen to him talk, but it's true."
- "Your father doesn't mean to embarrass you; he loves you children very, very much. He just has his own way of talking. . . . He means well; he really does!"
- "You're very lucky to have her for your doctor, you know. She's one of the top surgeons in the country! Never mind the way she talks—she doesn't mean any of it."

For the spouse of a touch dominant person, the translator role can become the major activity of life, as the spouse follows him or her around trying to explain, trying to repair the damage, trying to smooth things over. Trying, above all, to make it possible for other people to perceive the admirable person that the *spouse* knows is there underneath all the unsuccessful attempts at communication. The translator role is also commonly taken by people who work for touch dominant superiors, such as secretaries and receptionists and office nurses.

The touch dominant adult who doesn't have one of these translators has to struggle along alone, which often almost guarantees a lifetime of misunderstandings and loneliness. The TD adult who *does* have a translator goes through life feeling dependent on the person who provides that service, which adds nothing to his or her self-esteem and is a substantial emotional burden. It's never a good solution.

The Problems of Touch Dominant Adults

In Chapter Five we'll come back to this topic and discuss some measures that are more useful than just translation. For now, let's review the problems that TD adults have to face:

FIRST: They have all the problems that TD children have when they need to learn new information and acquire new skills. Unless they can find a hands-on learning situation, it takes them longer to get the material under control. And other people have a much lower tolerance for this characteristic in adults than in children, which leads to a great deal of friction.

SECOND: Like TD children, they are held back by the bias against touch language and the limitations on touch vocabulary. But children will only be fussed at and corrected; touch dominant teenagers and adults aren't that fortunate. *Their* heavy use of touch language is instead likely to be mistaken for sexual harassment, for verbal abuse, for profound ignorance or lack of intelligence, or for a completely antisocial attitude.

THIRD: In true emergencies—for example, when a loved one is injured and in an emergency room and the TD person is there trying to get information about what's happening—they tend to become locked into touch mode. This problem is temporary, but very real. In touch dominance lock it's hard for people either to speak or to understand the other sensory modes; it's almost impossible for them to remember the rules about "not being crude."

The struggle to find acceptable words is so frustrating that their normal ability to cope and communicate simply collapses. In these situations a problem that may ordinarily be little more than a nuisance can become serious, even tragic. Seemingly "out of control" behavior that would be tolerated from children in emergency situations will not be accepted from adults.

Our society is so touchy about these matters in the current environment of outrage over sexual abuse, sexual harassment, and epidemic violence that touch dominant persons in crisis are in danger of finding themselves wrongly perceived as villains or criminals. They are of course aware of this, which increases the stress and makes the touch dominance look worse, which intensifies the stress even more. And so on, around and around an ever more perilous loop.

FOURTH: Frequent rejection by others is no less painful for TD adults than it is for children. The adults have more power; they no longer have to worry about always "being in trouble," the way children do. But that advantage is more than outweighed by the fact that for them the rejection and misunderstanding have been going on for so long. Whatever labels they have acquired, whether those that come from experts—like "neurotic" or "borderline pesonality"—or those attached by the rest of us, which can be summarized as "a real pain in the neck," the terms have been attached for so long that everything they do is interpreted through the filter of the label. And most of the time, the TD adult has come to *believe* the label.

These problems all interact and have grave consequences. And people facing them must of course also deal with all the *other* problems that are part of daily life in this world. It takes tremendous strength and resilience for someone to grow up into an emotionally healthy and socially skilled adult while carrying such a burden. We should not be surprised by the fact that many touch dominant adults have just given up trying to fit in and have settled for being considered withdrawn or hostile or eccentric "loners."

Suppose the couple in Scenario Three had been aware of all of this information; would things have gone better for them?

Another Look at Scenario Three

The best way to change the outcome of this scenario would be for Jim Drake to do something about the potential misunderstanding *in advance*, by saying something like this to Melanie before she leaves for the hospital:

> "Honey, do me a favor, please: Remember to pay special attention to how Mom looks. I want to know whether she's wearing the new robe we bought for her. I want to know how her color is and whether she's smiling or not. I want to know how her eyes look. Those are the things that matter most to me, and I really need to know about them. All right?"

Given a specific list of items like this to watch for, Melanie will come home with the answers Jim wants. There will be no argument and no communication breakdown; Melanie will have no reason to feel that she needs to say anything like "I'm the stupid one in this family, remember?" It's not that she isn't capable of noticing and remembering visual information; it's just that unless she has a specific *reason* to do that, she will let data for the eye go by in favor of data that she perceives as being more important.

When we decide what parts of the flood of information coming at us we will choose to pay attention to and put indexes on for later retrieval from long-term memory storage, we have to rely on our *short*-term memory. Even when we're *not* under stress, its capacity is limited to roughly seven items at a time and roughly thirty seconds of storage; there's no way we can possibly process everything, or even a substantial part of it. Our natural tendency is to choose the items that go with our preferred sensory system and ignore the rest. This isn't part of our "character," it's just the way human memory works. But when we are alerted to an actual list of things to be remembered, like Jim's list for Melanie—and when the list is not made too long or too complicated—we have no trouble remembering those items instead.

I have often had people in my seminars say something like, "I shouldn't *have* to make a list! If she [or he] cared anything about me, that wouldn't be *necessary*!" That's absurd. Nobody has the limits of their short-term memory under conscious control. The more times someone is reminded of which items another person wants them to report on, the more likely they are to remember those items without being prompted. The day may come when the person will say, "And I know you'll want me to remember how things *look*—I promise not to forget." But refusing to help out by providing a list, especially when the other person will be under stress, is not a sensible strategy. It creates problems that can easily be avoided.

Workout Section Three

1. In a 1976 study reported by J. W. Prescott and Douglas Wallace, a survey of forty-nine nonliterate cultures found—for forty-seven of the forty-nine—that there was an overwhelming correlation between violence and the culture's tolerance for touch. The higher the amount of tactile experience allowed, the less violent the culture was. We are a *literate* culture, but we are strongly biased against touch and are suffering an overwhelming epidemic of violence. Do you think this is significant?

2. The proposed tree structure shown in Figure 1 sets out different divisions of touch. Do you think it's adequate? Would you make changes?

3. It's not unusual for eye and ear dominant people to tell me that they flat-out don't *believe* that anybody actually uses touch language very much—not real people, not in the real world. To demonstrate that that's not true, here are a set of touch language quotations from a variety of sources.

   a. "But for the grace of God we would have got in some quicksand that would have sunk Sonic." (J. Vernon

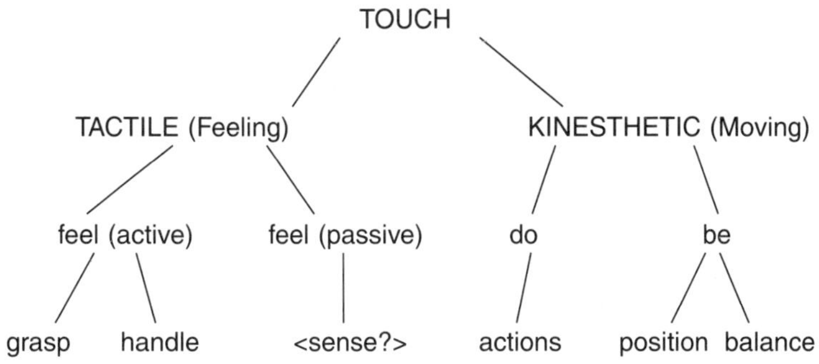

Figure 1

Stewart, quoted in "People Talk Thin but Eat Fat," by Seth Lubove, *Forbes,* July 10, 1992; on page 307.)

b. "If you own shares of a hot little concept company and you're counting on press releases and crowd psychology to push the stock higher (or keep it from drifting lower), my advice is to think very seriously about getting out while you still can." (Frederick E. Rose, Jr., "Weasel Words," *Forbes,* December 23, 1991; on page 184.)

c. "In a crash, my Brooklyn neighbors were inclined to believe, such trading would give a plunging human investor little in the way of an outcropping to grab onto, or a level terrace on which to rest, recuperate, and, above all, think." (L. J. Davis, "The Next Panic," *Harper's Magazine,* May 1991; on page 39.)

d. "If the poor believe that most wealthy people are exploiters and thieves who squash other people into poverty for personal gain, they will not be likely to climb the ladder of economic success." (Michael Bauman, "The Dangerous Samaritans: How We Unintentionally Injure the Poor," *Imprimis,* January 1994; on page 4.)

e. "When I get this anxiety state I cannot walk further. I run into myself. It breaks me into pieces. I am like a spray. I lose my center of gravity. I have no weight. . . . I need something to hold me together." (A woman patient, quoted in *The Woman in the Body: A Cultural Analysis of Reproduction,* by Emily Martin, Beacon Press 1987; on page 75.)

Touchpoints

It's hard for touch dominant people to find good writing in touch language that is neither violent nor pornographic. We need collections of nonviolent reading materials with heavily tactile vocabularies. Here are a few examples of the sort of thing I mean; you might begin a collection of your own.

1. "With my index finger dripping brake fluid . . . I delicately assess the bore of a brake cylinder. I am feeling for pits in the metal that could render it unfit for further service. . . . I am alone with my customer's life in the narrow span of my greasy palm."

   (Don Sharp, "Aristotle's Garage: A Mechanic's Metaphysics," *Harper's Magazine,* March 1981, pp. 91–93; on pp. 91–92.)

2. "At last he takes her hand, raising it in both of his own. Now he bends over the bed in a kind of crouching stance, his head drawn down into the collar of his robe. His eyes are closed as he feels for her pulse. In a moment he has found the spot, and for the next half hour he remains thus . . . holding the pulse of the woman beneath his fingers, cradling her hand in his."

   (Richard Selzer, "The Art of Surgery: Trespassing on Sacred Ground," *Harper's Magazine,* January 1976, pp. 75–78; on p. 78. He is writing about his observation of the Dalai Lama's personal physician taking a pulse. It's worth noting that Chinese patients often talk about visits to the doctor as "going to have my pulse felt"; in the United States, on the other hand, we "go see a doctor" and are told, "The doctor will see you now.")

3. "When you write, you lay out a line of words. The line of words is a miner's pick, a woodcarver's gouge, a surgeon's probe. You wield it, and it digs a path you follow."

   (Annie Dillard, on p. 3 of *The Writing Life*, Harper & Row 1989.)

4. "Up to your shoulder inside a cow, you feel the hot heavy squeeze of her, but I'll never forget my startled delight the first time I withdrew my hand slowly and felt the cow's muscles contract and release me one after another, like a row of people shaking hands with me in a receiving line. I wonder if this is how it feels to be born."

   (Diane Ackerman, *A Natural History of the Senses,* Random House 1990, p. 81. One of the best sources of information about touch, and about all the other senses as well.)

Talking Touch

1. People you get along with may . . .

touch your heart	have a magic touch
warm your heart	give you a pat on the back
give you a hand up	tickle you
hit it off with you	put themselves in your place
get solidly behind you	give you a leg up
back you up	follow your lead
reach out to you	touch you deeply
be handy to have around	stick their necks out for you

cut you some slack	try to be flexible
let you lean on them	stand by you

2. People you don't get along with may . . .

rub you the wrong way	make your skin crawl
give you a bad feeling	be cold fish
lack the personal touch	thumb their noses at you
make you lose your grip	try to pick on you
give you itchy feet	make you feel numb
give you the creeps	brush you off
push you too far	get under your skin
let you down	pull the rug out from under you
go behind your back	sweep your ideas under the rug
make your blood boil	give you a pain in the neck

3. Some people are . . .

thick-skinned	touchy	thin-skinned
pushy	overbearing	soft touches
stiff and rigid	crusty	smooth and slick
hard-hearted	soft-hearted	warm-hearted
cold-hearted	unbalanced	hard to deal with
cool toward others	flaky	crooked
down to earth	stuck-up	stiff-necked